To my beloved daughters, whose laughter fills my days with joy and whose curiosity inspires me to see the world through fresh eyes. To my dear grandma, who has believed in me and has been a guiding light. Your love and support have been my motivation, and I carry your spirit with me in every word I write. This book is a tribute to your enduring love and encouragement.

Love, Pauline

Library of Congress Control Number: 2024910382
Printed in China.

ISBN: 979-8-218-43255-3
Text by Pauline Kimsoung
Artwork by Quynh Rua
Edited by Duck Duck Publishing
Book designed by Duck Duck Publishing
First Edition 2024

Sweet Durian Stories
Chelmsford, MA
United States of America

My Cambodian-American New Year

A Celebration of Love and Traditions

Written by
Pauline Kimsoung

Illustrated by
Nguyen Phuong Quynh

SWEET DURIAN STORIES
BY PAULINE KIMSOUNG

In my family, we celebrate two New Year's.

on December 31st

One takes place on December 31st.
The other takes place from April 13th to April 15th.

from April 13th to April 15th

Let's explore the magic of both
American and Cambodian New Year!

On December 31st, New Year's Eve,
we head to Yeay's house for a night full of fun.

We wear cozy pajamas. We get to stay past our bedtime.
Board games, laughter, and sparkling cider fill up the night while
we create lasting memories with blended traditions!

Just like Thanksgiving, our family gathers around
for a tasty feast of fried rice, egg rolls, and
lo mein – my favorite mixed noodles.

We share what we are grateful for:
our family, our health, and memorable
moments from the past year.

For dessert, it's strawberry shortcake! We love baking with Yeay. The scents fill our home. It feels so warm and cozy.

It's not just the warmth of the food, but the warmth of family together that makes the celebration complete.

After dinner, we always play Klah Klok! In Klah Klok,
instead of dots, each side of the dice has pictures.
Players take guesses about which pictures will show up as
the dice roll. We place bets as the dice spin into a bowl.

It's a game filled with wonder and endless possibilities.

When the clock strikes midnight on December 31st, we shout "Happy New Year!"

HAPPY NEW YEAR

We cheer, drink sparkling cider, and watch the fireworks explode on TV as we hope for a bright new year!

On April 13th, it's the Cambodian New Year! The Khmer calendar says it's time to clean the house and display flowers and food at our family altar.

The altar honors our family's protecting spirit.

For breakfast, we prepare kuyteav –
rice noodles in a delicious beef broth
with lots of tasty toppings. We eat noodles
on special occasions like New Year's Day
because noodles mean having a long life!

As part of our celebration, we share our home cooked meals with the monks at the temple. Sharing food is our way of saying thank you.

We use a special food carrier called Chan Srak. It's made of metal and has tiers of deep bowls.

What makes a Chan Srak beautiful is the Cambodian artwork handcrafted onto the metal. It plays a big role in bringing offerings to the monks, just like our ancestors did.

It's like a treasure chest filled with surprises!

Now it's time to
head to the temple.

The beautiful temple is a sacred place where dragons crafted from gold
dance along the railings. Cambodian letters spell "The Peace Meditation Center",
and beside the stairs stands a big gold Buddha statue, smiling warmly.

As we listen to the monks' gentle chanting, we take a moment to remember and honor our ancestors. It makes our hearts feel warm and happy to connect with our past and receive blessings for our future.

Back home, it's time for a feast! A few of our favorite Cambodian dishes are Cha Ma Sur, Salaw Machu Kroeung, and mouthwatering Num Ansom Chek.

Cha Ma Sur is stir-fried vermicelli noodles with fish sauce. It often includes pork, mushrooms, and tofu skin.

Salaw Machu Kroeung is a sour beef soup. It's made with celery and green beans.

It sure is *spicy!*

Num Ansom Chek is a banana rice cake. It is made of sticky rice, shredded coconut, and bananas.

It is so fun to eat because we have to unwrap it like a present!

So, whether it's December or April, our celebrations blend both cultures together like a beautiful painting with a multitude of colors. We get double the laughter, love, and joy.

Thanks to our great-grandparents who brought these rich traditions to our family, we love seeing American and Cambodian traditions come together every year!

Glossary

Ma	Mom
Pa	Dad
Yeay	Grandma
Tha	Grandpa
Num Ansom Chek	A banana rice cake dessert
Salaw Machu Kroeung	A sour beef soup with lemongrass paste, celery and green beans.
Cha Ma Sur	A stir-fried vermicelli noodles served with sweet fish sauce
Chan Srak	A special metal food carrier with tiers of deep bowls.
Kuyteav	Also known as Pho, rice noodles in a delicious beef broth with lots of tasty toppings.

Reference:
Pann Rethea. (2019, September 08). Craftsmen strive to keep the ancient art of food container-making alive. The Phnom Penh Post. https://m.phnompenhpost.com/lifestyle-arts-culture/craftmen-strive-keep-ancient-art-food-container-making-alive

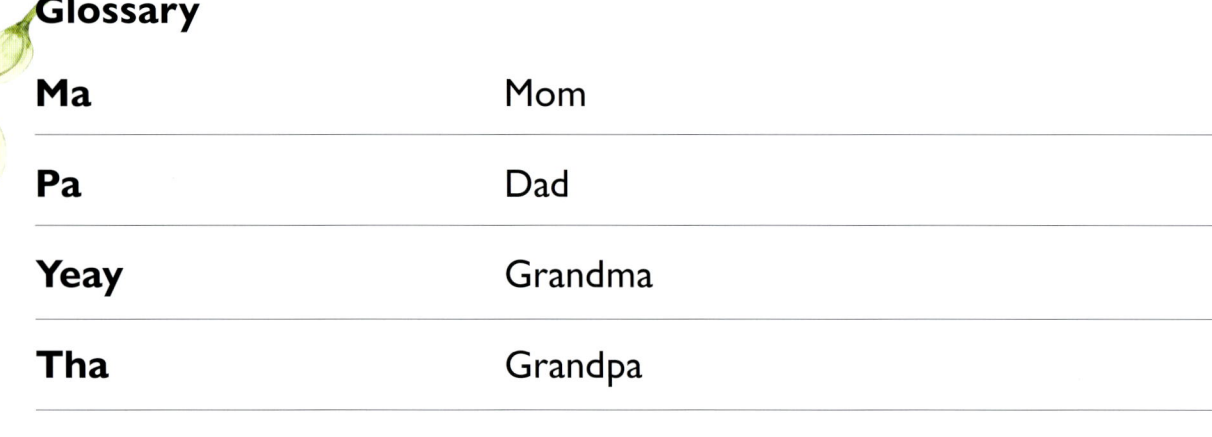

About the Author

Hey there, I'm Pauline Kimsoung, a computer science teacher from Chelmsford, MA, and a wife and mom to two amazing daughters. Our home is a joyful chaos with our two dogs, Rosie & Penni, and our two cats, Max & Basil, keeping us on our toes.

When I'm not teaching, I'm diving into books and chasing my dream of writing children's stories. Growing up, I wished for books that celebrated my Cambodian roots, so now I'm on a mission to fill that gap.

Family time is my favorite, whether it's exploring nature, or just hanging out at home. With every story I write, I hope to spread love, acceptance, and a whole lot of fun.

About the Illustrator

Hey there, I'm Nguyen Phuong Quynh, but my friends call me Quynh Rua. I'm an illustrator based in Vietnam, with almost a decade of experience. I specialize in bringing stories to life through illustrations, focusing on children's books, character design, and handmade artwork.

I'm all about attention to detail and making sure every project exceeds expectations. I adore creating cute and whimsical illustrations that enchant young readers. For me, visuals are key to enhancing storytelling and forging connections between authors and their audience.

Outside of illustration, I love crafting, getting lost in a good book and enjoying a leisurely walk. I also love spending time with my family and sharing delicious food.